MW00329259

THE TRUTH ABOUT STYLE

ABRAMS NOTERIE, NEW YORK

CON TENTS

*STYLE IS
SERIOUS
BUT DOES
NOT TAKE
ITSELF
SERIOUSLY.*

The merciless arbiter of fashion enjoys dividing the world into two distinct groups: those who are born with style and those who are not. That is, one either has it or never will. But they are mistaken—even if style is not in our genes, it is omnipresent throughout our lives. Similar to learning a language, mastering a sense of style can be easy, chaotic, or painful. Because style looks beyond imposed rules, seasonal trends, hip vocabulary, the length of hems, and of-the-moment heel shapes. Style is far more than a dress code, a chic logo, or a price tag on a clothing label. It is audacity, originality, disobedience, and errors of taste. It is living matter. We massage it, we manipulate it, we turn it in all directions.

"Can you help me find my style?" "Do you think I could be a woman whom others see as having style?" "Can one have style without following fashion?" Every day, as a personal stylist, I try to help answer these questions for men and women who appreciate the importance of having a wardrobe that reflects them, but who understand nothing of the conflicting rules of trends. And more so, how do any of us compete with catwalk goddesses and young, carefree influencers when we find ourselves with too much thigh, not enough leg, too much stomach, not enough chest, and far too much puffiness under the eyes?

Yet style does not care for age or measurements. Style cares not whether we own a little black dress and red-soled shoes. Style is concerned exclusively with us. With our desire to play, our daily mood, our whims, our days with and our days without . . . No extravagance is necessary to have style, and one can cultivate a subtle look without succumbing to blandness. But even when it appears obvious, style demands reflection. "Effortless chic" does not exist. It requires practice. "I threw on the first thing I saw" is nothing but a ploy to elicit compliments. In fact, if style is indeed within everyone's reach, it still requires a minimum level of creativity to assemble clothes, to juxtapose muted and intense colors, to mix restrained prints with punchy ones, and to play with combinations—a teenager's hoodie, say, beneath an elegant coat; a pencil skirt with men's sneakers;

a fitted blazer over a bohemian dress. And true style has the good taste to reveal itself in the details: fishnet ankle socks with heels, a large rhinestone brooch on a khaki parka, a flowery blouse with a business suit. The playing field is vast!

To have style is to respect those days when we lack the desire to display ourselves, and then to bring out the sequins when they call to us, be it day or night. It is to play with a look that is not entirely ours. It is to try. And to fail. To change our minds while listening only to ourselves. Style is serious but does not take itself seriously. It supports us in what we do and say each day. It makes us smile, it surprises and reassures us, and it delights those who love us.

—ISABELLE THOMAS, Author of *Paris Street Style*

WHAT IS

STYLE?

Style is as unique as the
choices we make every
morning when we get
dressed. It's who we are,
it's how we feel, it's what
we show the world each
day—that's style.

Fashion can be
bought. Style one
must possess.

-EDNA WOOLMAN
CHASE

The difference
between style and
fashion is quality.

-GIORGIO ARMANI

Fashion passes.
Style remains.

-COCO CHANEL

Fashion is about dressing according to what's fashionable. Style is more about being yourself.

—OSCAR DE LA RENTA

STYLE IS . . .

. . . the principle of decision in a work of art.

—*SUSAN SONTAG*

. . . saying complicated things in a simple way.

—*JEAN COCTEAU*

. . . joyful if you allow yourself to have joy.

—*STACY LONDON*

. . . the substance of the subject called unceasingly
to the surface.

—*VICTOR HUGO*

. . . the perfection of a point of view.

—*RICHARD EBERHART*

. . . a deeply personal expression of who you are,
and every time you dress, you are asserting a part
of yourself.

—*NINA GARCÍA*

I think there are very few people who have a real style, a real personality, and real beauty.

—*MARISA BERENSON*

Style is character.

—*JOAN DIDION*

Style is not neutral. It gives moral directions.

—*MARTIN AMIS*

For me, style is matter.

—*VLADIMIR NABOKOV*

Ironically, style doesn't come even closely related to fashion. . . . You can take it to a philosophical level: Style is about the choices you make to create the aspects of civilization that you wish to uphold.

—DAVID BOWIE

To be truly stylish (as opposed to merely "in style," which is the opposite) is to be unabashedly one's self, without reference to the fashions and demands of a sweltering crowd.

—MICHAEL HARRIS

If you have a sense of style and purpose
and will you don't want to compromise.

—*VIDAL SASSOON*

Real style is never right or wrong.
It's a matter of being yourself. On purpose.

—*G. BRUCE BOYER*

You do not create a style. You work,
and develop yourself; your style is
an emanation from your own being.

—*KATHERINE ANNE PORTER*

I admire anyone with their own sense
of personal style.

—NICOLE RICHIE

Talent and taste are not enough.
Only style counts.

—PIERRE CARDIN

Taste has no system and no proofs.

—SUSAN SONTAG

Style is the answer to everything—
A fresh way to approach a dull or
a dangerous thing

To do a dull thing with style
is preferable to doing a dangerous
thing without it

To do a dangerous thing with style
is what I call art

—*CHARLES BUKOWSKI*

I dress for the image. Not for myself,
not for the public, not for fashion, not for men.

—MARLENE DIETRICH

What's my style is not your style.

—IRIS APFEL

The kind of style I am thinking about is a
projection of personality and you have to
have a personality before you can project it.

—RAYMOND CHANDLER

RENÉ
LACOSTE

THE

ALLI-GATOR

René Lacoste was a renowned tennis player in the 1920s, winning a few singles titles such as Wimbledon and the U.S. National Championship. In 1927, he was nicknamed "the Alligator" after having made a bet with an opponent over an alligator-skin suitcase. After he returned to France, the Alligator eventually became the Crocodile, and Lacoste was known as such ever after. He went on to have a friend's drawing of a crocodile embroidered on a blazer he wore on the court. Later, in 1933, Lacoste designed the first modern short-sleeve tennis shirt, which would revolutionize sports clothing, and had it emblazoned with the crocodile.

In matters of great importance,
style, not sincerity, is the vital thing.

—OSCAR WILDE
THE IMPORTANCE OF BEING EARNEST

Self-plagiarism is style.

—ALFRED HITCHCOCK

I might say that what amateurs call a style is
usually only the unavoidable awkwardnesses
in first trying to make something that has not
heretofore been made.

—ERNEST HEMINGWAY

He has found his style, when he cannot
do otherwise.

—PAUL KLEE

When you look at iconic people, most of the
time they are dressed up exactly the same way
for all their life. They dress for themselves.

—ISABEL MARANT

It's important to find what really suits who you
are, because style isn't only what you wear,
it's what you project.

—CAROLINA HERRERA

Style is not something applied. It is something that permeates. It is of the nature of that in which it is found, whether the poem, the manner of a god, the bearing of a man. It is not a dress.

—*WALLACE STEVENS*

For me, style is a state of mind and individuality.

—TIGER SHROFF

Style is the only thing you can't buy. It's not in a shopping bag, a label, or a price tag. It's something reflected from our soul to the outside world—an emotion.

—ALBER ELBAZ

Style is knowing who you are, what you want to say, and not giving a damn.

—ORSON WELLES

Fashion says, "Me, too," and style, "Only me."

—*GERALDINE STUTZ*

Fashion is what you're offered four times a year
by designers. And style is what you choose.

—*LAUREN HUTTON*

"Fashion" is what designers create and sell. . . .
"Style" is your usage and interpretation of
what is available to you.

—*CLINTON KELLY*

Style doesn't have seasons.

—*POLLY ALLEN MELLEN*

Fashion is OK for five days, one minute,
six months, but style is for the rest of the life.

—*STEFANO GABBANA*

Oh, never mind the fashion. When one has a
style of one's own, it is always twenty times better.

—*MARGARET OLIPHANT*
MISS MARJORIBANKS

" You know, Minister, I disagree with
Dumbledore on many counts . . .
but you cannot deny he's got style."

—*J. K. ROWLING*
**HARRY POTTER AND THE
ORDER OF THE PHOENIX**

Joan of Arc had style. Jesus had style.

—*CHARLES BUKOWSKI*
PORTIONS FROM A
WINE-STAINED NOTEBOOK

STYLE...

. . . used to be an interaction between the human soul and tools that were limiting. In the digital era, it will have to come from the soul alone.

—JARON LANIER

. . . really comes down to what makes you feel good.

—ALEXANDRA STODDARD

. . . is a matter of taste, design a matter of principle.

—THOMAS CHURCH

. . . is the dress of thoughts.

—LORD CHESTERFIELD

. . . applies to everything you do.

—DAVID BOWIE

I f you look back in history of the women who are most memorable and most stylish, they were never the followers of fashion. They were the ones who were unique in their style, breakers of the rules. They were authentic, genuine, original. They were not following the trends.

—*NINA GARCÍA*

Find your own style.
Don't spend your
savings trying to be
someone else. You're
not more important,
smarter, or prettier
because you wear a
designer dress.

—*SALMA HAYEK*

To achieve style, begin
by affecting none.

—*WILLIAM STRUNK JR.
AND E. B. WHITE*
THE ELEMENTS OF STYLE

All styles are good
except the tiresome
kind.

—*VOLTAIRE*

Style reflects one's
idiosyncrasies. Your
personality is apt to
show more to the
degree that you did
not solve the problem
than to the degree
that you did.

—*CHARLES EAMES*

COCO
CHANEL

NO PRACTICAL

WAY TO RIDE A

HORSE

Coco Chanel was known for a silhouette, perfume, and style of jewelry all so iconic they're still impactful today. But she also made great strides for women's fashion, shortening skirts so that ankles were in full view, wearing pants to make traveling easier, and publically acknowledging that there was, in fact, no practical way to ride a horse if you were wearing a skirt.

I believe that if
you think about
what style means,
you won't become
a fashion victim.

—*JOHN VARVATOS*

Style is the shape the
ideal takes, rhythm,
its movement.

—*VICTOR HUGO*
LES MISÉRABLES

A man's style is
intrinsic and private
with him like his
voice or his gesture,
partly a matter of
inheritance, partly of
cultivation. It is the
pattern of the soul.

—*MAURICE VALENCY*

My number-one
theory in life is that
style is proportional
to your lack of
resources—the less
you have, the more
stylish you're likely
to be.

—*BETH DITTO*

1. Find your own style and have the courage to stick to it.

2. Choose your clothes for your way of life.

3. Make your wardrobe as versatile as an actress. It should be able to play many roles.

4. Find your happiest colors—the ones that make you feel good.

5. Care for your clothes, like the good friends they are!

—JOAN CRAWFORD

I'm not fashionable, and I know nothing about fashion, but I have my individual style, and style is eternal.

—*VIDYA BALAN*

WHAT IS

FASHION?

Our personality, our
virtues, our values—
it's what's on the inside
that counts. But there's
certainly a lot to be
said for what we choose
to wear on the outside.

Fashion is very important. It is life-enhancing and, like everything else that gives pleasure, it is worth doing well.

—*VIVIENNE WESTWOOD*

Art, literature, entertainment, travel, politics, décor, food, and dress are expressions of everyday living and of common interest to men and women alike.

—*FLEUR COWLES*

Fashion is so close in revealing a person's inner feelings and everybody seems to hate to lay claim to vanity so people tend to push it away. It's really too close to the quick of the soul.

—*STELLA BLUM*

Fashion is not necessarily about labels.
It's not about brands. It's about something
else that comes from within you.

—RALPH LAUREN

What you wear is such an expression of who
you are. Working with a stylist would be like
someone picking out who I'm going to date!

—DIANE KRUGER

It's not about following the trends,
it's about creating something inspired.

—JANIE BRYANT

Clothing . . . is at once science, art, habit, and feeling.

—*HONORÉ DE BALZAC*

Clothes are like a good meal, a good movie, great pieces of music.

—*MICHAEL KORS*

Fashion is only the attempt to realize art in living forms and social intercourse.

—*OLIVER WENDELL HOLMES JR.*

The secret of fashion is to surprise and never to disappoint.

—*EDWARD BULWER-LYTTON*

If you can't eat it, it's not food,
and if you can't wear it, it's not fashion,
it is something else.

—ALBER ELBAZ

Sometimes comfort doesn't matter.
When a shoe is freakin' fabulous, it may
be worth a subsequent day of misery.
Soak in Epsom salts and take comfort in the
fact that you're better than everyone else.

—*CLINTON KELLY*

You can never take too much care over the choice of your shoes. Too many women think that they are unimportant, but the real proof of any elegant woman is what is on their feet.

—*CHRISTIAN DIOR*

Shoes transform your body language and attitude. They lift you physically and emotionally.

—*CHRISTIAN LOUBOUTIN*

To be well dressed is a little like being in love.

—OLEG CASSINI

The dress must follow the body of a woman,
not the body following the shape of the dress.

—HUBERT DE GIVENCHY

You are only as good as the people you dress.

—HALSTON

Certain dressmakers desire to pass for an artist.
I have one ambition: that is to have good taste.

—JEAN PATOU

Whenever I sign a garment with my name,
I consider myself as the creator of the masterpiece.

—PAUL POIRET

woman's best dress should be like a
barbed-wire fence, serving its purpose
without obstructing the view.

—SOPHIA LOREN

Your dresses should be tight enough to show you're a woman and loose enough to show you're a lady.

—EDITH HEAD

AUDREY
HEPBURN

DÉ-
COLLLETÉ

SAB-
RINA

In 1953, young fashion designer Hubert de Givenchy received a phone call from Gladys de Segonzac, the director of Schiaparelli: "Miss Hepburn" wanted to meet de Givenchy at once. Pre-*Roman Holiday* fame, and therefore not the Katherine Hepburn that de Givenchy was expecting, Audrey Hepburn, "this very thin person with beautiful eyes, short hair, thick eyebrows, very tiny trousers, ballerina shoes, and a little T-shirt," arrived and charmed the Paris fashion designer. She selected several outfits of his that she would go on to wear in *Sabrina*, including a black cocktail dress with a full ballerina-length skirt and bows at the shoulders, introducing a style now known as "décolleté Sabrina" to the world.

Must I make myself a slave to fashion
And not dress for my own sake?

—MOLIÈRE
THE SCHOOL OF HUSBANDS

It is useless to dabble in beauty.
One must be utterly devoted to beauty,
with every nerve of the body.

—ANNA PAVLOVA

I prefer imperfections—it's much more
interesting. Perfect is boring.

—GRACE CODDINGTON

You Don't Have to Be Pretty.
You don't owe prettiness to anyone.

—ERIN MCKEAN

For something to be beautiful
it doesn't have to be pretty.

—REI KAWAKUBO

I always find beauty in things that are odd and
imperfect. They are so much more interesting.

—MARC JACOBS

design clothes because I don't want women to look all innocent and naïve. I want women to look stronger. I don't like women to be taken advantage of. I don't like men whistling at women in the street. I think they deserve more respect . . . I want to empower women. I want people to be afraid of the women I dress.

—ALEXANDER MCQUEEN

It is true that I am rather taken up with dress;
but as to feathers, everyone wears them, and
it would seem extraordinary if I did not.

—*MARIE ANTOINETTE*

A great dress can make you remember
what is beautiful about life.

—*RACHEL ROY*

I think women will never lose that appetite for
fashion. I think women want to look beautiful.
I think that's an important thing. It is relevant.

—*TORY BURCH*

Clothes don't make a man, but clothes have got many a man a good job.

—HERBERT HAROLD VREELAND

Clothes and manners do not make the man; but when he is made, they greatly improve his appearance.

—HENRY WARD BEECHER

While clothes may not make the woman, they certainly have a strong effect on her self-confidence—which, I believe, does make the woman.

—MARY KAY ASH

People can say, "What do you mean you want to help the world, and you're so concerned about fashion?" It's illegal to be naked. . . . That is something that is extremely important.

—*KANYE WEST*

One-third of your life is spent in bed, two-thirds of your life in clothes.

—*E. L. BRENTLINGER*

How can you live the high life if you do not
wear the high heels?

—SONIA RYKIEL

Men tell me that I've saved their marriages.
It costs them a fortune in shoes, but it's cheaper
than a divorce.

—MANOLO BLAHNIK

Beauty is a pair of shoes that makes you wanna die.

—FRANK ZAPPA

I have always loved fashion because it's a great way to express your mood. And I'm definitely a shoe lover. The right pair of shoes can change the feel of an outfit, and even change how a woman feels about herself. A woman can wear confidence on her feet with a high stiletto, or slip into weekend comfort with a soft ballet flat.

—FERGIE

Fashion should be stylish and fun.

—TWIGGY

For us, fashion is an antidote to reality.

—VIKTOR & ROLF

Fashion is all about happiness. It's fun.
It's important. But it's not medicine.

—DONATELLA VERSACE

You either know fashion or you don't.

—*ANNA WINTOUR*

I don't do fashion. I am fashion.

—*COCO CHANEL*

I don't approach fashion. Fashion approaches me.

—*DAPHNE GUINNESS*

Miranda: "You have no style or sense of fashion."

Andy: "Well, I think that depends on—"

Miranda: "No, no, that wasn't a question."

—*THE DEVIL WEARS PRADA*

It's a new challenge to see how people can change your look. I like words like transformation, reinvention, and chameleon. Because one word I don't like is predictable.

—*NAOMI CAMPBELL*

A woman would be in despair if Nature had formed her as fashion makes her appear.

—*MLLE. DE LESPINASSE*

Fashion is more usually a gentle progression of revisited ideas.

—*BRUCE OLDFIELD*

Even I don't wake up looking like Cindy Crawford.

—*CINDY CRAWFORD*

Looking a certain way is a blessing and a curse.

—*FARRAH FAWCETT*

"Style" is an expression of individualism mixed with charisma. Fashion is something that comes after style.

—*JOHN FAIRCHILD*

Fashion wasn't what you wore someplace anymore; it was the whole reason for going.

—*ANDY WARHOL*

Those who make their dress a principal part of themselves, will, in general, become of no more value than their dress.

—*WILLIAM HAZLITT*

Don't just eat McDonald's, get something a bit better. Eat a salad. That's what fashion is. It's something that is a bit better.

—*VIVIENNE WESTWOOD*

I love new clothes. If everyone could just wear new clothes every day, I reckon depression wouldn't exist anymore.

—*SOPHIE KINSELLA*
CONFESSIONS OF A SHOPAHOLIC

Fashion is ridiculous before and after; it's only tolerable during.

—*PIERRE CARDIN*

I love fashion, and I love changing my style, my hair, my makeup, and everything I've done in the past has made me what I am now. Not everyone is going to like what I do, but I look back at everything, and it makes me smile.

—*VICTORIA BECKHAM*

think fashion is a lot of fun. I love clothes. More than fashion or brand labels, I love design. I love the thought that people put into clothes. I love when clothes make cultural statements and I think personal style is really cool. I also freely recognize that fashion should be a hobby.

—*ANNE HATHAWAY*

Architecture is how the person places herself
in the space. Fashion is about how you place
the object on the person.

—ZAHA HADID

Fashion is the science of appearances,
and it inspires one with the desire to seem
rather than to be.

—EDWIN HUBBELL CHAPIN

When I see beautiful clothes, I want to
keep them, preserve them. . . . Clothes, like
architecture and art, reflect an era.

—AZZEDINE ALAÏA

THE INAU-GURAL *SUIT*

PRESIDENT GEORGE WASHINGTON

On the day of his inauguration, George Washington wore clothing that supported and reflected the new country he was being sworn in to lead. He wore brown wool cloth made in America, preferring it to clothing that up until that point had always come from Britain, and each of his buttons was emblazoned with an eagle, an ode to the new symbol of the United States.

When in doubt, wear red.

—*BILL BLASS*

There is no blue without yellow and without orange.

—*VINCENT VAN GOGH*

Some people hate lime-green; red has
all this emotional baggage. Blue seems
to be overall one of the more positive colors,
and a little more serious than yellow.

—*DAVID CARSON*

I wear black because I'm comfortable in it. But then in the summertime when it's hot I'm comfortable in light blue.

—*JOHNNY CASH*

I don't design clothes. I design dreams.

—*RALPH LAUREN*

Fashion is about change and, for me,
the philosophy is always the same . . .
that the clothes have to be really modern
and make women look really beautiful.

—*CALVIN KLEIN*

If I can have any impact, I want women to feel
good about themselves and have fun with fashion.

—*MICHELLE OBAMA*

design for the woman I wanted to be, the woman I used to be, and to some degree, the woman I'm still a little piece of.

—*DIANE VON FURSTENBERG*

Tai: "Do you think she's pretty?"

Cher: "She's a full-on Monet."

Tai: "What's a Monet?"

Cher: "It's like the paintings, see? From far away
        it's OK, but up close it's a big old mess."

—CLUELESS

I'm also interested in seeing just the girl on the street, because she is unlike any other. I'm inspired by whatever it is she might be wearing.

—*ANNA WINTOUR*

The best fashion show is definitely on the street. Always has been, and always will be.

—*BILL CUNNINGHAM*

I like my money right where I can see it:
hanging in my closet.

—*CARRIE BRADSHAW*
SEX AND THE CITY

Whoever said money can't buy happiness
simply didn't know where to go shopping.

—*BO DEREK*

"They're such beautiful shirts," she sobbed, her voice muffled in the thick folds. "It makes me sad because I've never seen such— such beautiful shirts before."

—*F. SCOTT FITZGERALD*
THE GREAT GATSBY

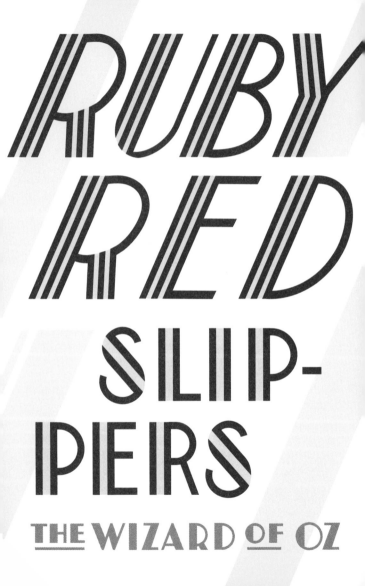

RUBY RED SLIP-PIERS

THE WIZARD OF OZ

In L. Frank Baum's novel *The Wizard of Oz*, Dorothy wore silver slippers. But for the 1939 film adaptation the filmmakers chose to make them ruby red instead, as the very nature of a color film was so exciting that a bold color choice was warranted. To celebrate the fiftieth anniversary of the film in 1989, Ronald Winston, of the celebrated jewelers the House of Harry Winston, created a pair of real ruby slippers with more than four thousand rubies. They are the most expensive pair of shoes in the world.

I think everyone loves a slash of red lipstick.

—*GWENDOLINE CHRISTIE*

The shiny red color of the soles has no function other than to identify to the public that they are mine. I selected the color because it is engaging, flirtatious, memorable, and the color of passion.

—*CHRISTIAN LOUBOUTIN*

I wish I had invented blue jeans.

—*YVES SAINT LAURENT*

I want to die with my blue jeans on.

—*ANDY WARHOL*

B ut when I fell in love with black,
it contained all color. It wasn't a negation
of color. It was an acceptance. Because
black encompasses all colors. Black is the most
aristocratic color of all . . . You can be quiet,
and it contains the whole thing.

—LOUISE NEVELSON

The little black dress is the hardest thing
to realize because you must keep it simple.

—*HUBERT DE GIVENCHY*

I'll stop wearing black when they invent
a darker color.

—*EMMANUELLE ALT*

What you wear is how you present yourself to the world, especially today, when human contacts are so quick. Fashion is instant language.

—MIUCCIA PRADA

Fashion is a tool . . . to compete in life outside the home. People like you better, without knowing why, because people always react well to a person they like the looks of.

—MARY QUANT

Clothes and courage have much to do with each other.

—SARA JEANNETTE DUNCAN

Beauty, by way of
fashion, has to do
with confidence, with
flattering silhouettes,
with patterns, with
proper fit for body
type, and with an
abundance of self-love!

—*MARY LAMBERT*

Keep it simple.
You don't want to
overdo it with too
much makeup or
crazy, over-the-top
hairstyles. Let your
natural beauty show
through.

—*HEIDI KLUM*

Looking good
isn't self-importance;
it's self-respect.

—*CHARLES HIX*

Diamonds are a girl's best friend, and dogs are a man's best friend. Now you know which sex has more sense.

—*ZSA ZSA GABOR*

My style is not that big. I wear heels, tight pants, and I wear diamonds.

—*DONATELLA VERSACE*

Let us not be too particular; it is better to have old secondhand diamonds than none at all.

—*MARK TWAIN*

I never worry about diets. The only carrots that interest me are the number of carats in diamonds.

—*MAE WEST*

I dress in my "uniform," or my own dress code, which reflects my personal method and work ethic. My belief is that my plain T-shirt—I have about 40 of them—or blue sweater helps focus others' attention on me and on what I say.

—GIORGIO ARMANI

When you're young, the blue blazer feels like a grown-up costume.

—WILLIE GEIST

I have always been a romantic, one of those people who believes that a woman in pink circus tights contains all the secrets of the universe.

—*TOM ROBBINS*

My parents told me I'd point to a bed of flowers and say "Pink. Pretty," before I knew any other words.

—*JONI MITCHELL*

was preppy, then suddenly switched around age fourteen. I asked my mother to go to this vintage store, and she let me buy a leopard swing coat, pink cigarette pants, and lime-green gloves.

—KATE SPADE

Fashion is like eating, you shouldn't stick
to the same menu.

—KENZŌ TAKADA

My attitude is if fashion says it's forbidden,
I'm going to do it.

—MICHAEL JACKSON

Evening is a time of real experimentation.
You never want to look the same way.

—DONNA KARAN

With a black pullover and ten rows of pearls,
Chanel revolutionized fashion.

—*CHRISTIAN DIOR*

I'm just trying to change the world one sequin
at a time.

—*LADY GAGA*

I wanted to live like a colorful butterfly in the sun.

—*MATA HARI*

He was struck again by the religious reverence of even the most unworldly American women for the social advantages of dress. "It's their armour," he thought, "their defence against the unknown, and their defiance of it." And he understood for the first time the earnestness with which May, who was incapable of tying a ribbon in her hair to charm him, had gone through the solemn rite of selecting and ordering her extensive wardrobe.

—*EDITH WHARTON*
THE AGE OF INNOCENCE

Always have a pink Oxford shirt ready for days when you're feeling run down.

—MICHAEL BASTIAN

Red is the ultimate cure for sadness.

—BILL BLASS

Fashion is that thing that saved me from being sad.

—LADY GAGA

GYPSY
ROSE LEE

THE

HATS

LOOK So

NAKED

In the spring of 1955 her friend Mr. John, the famous milliner, showed her his spring collection in advance. Gypsy bought one of the hats, took it apart, made a dozen copies, and distributed them to her friends as Easter gifts. Mr. John noticed one of these friends, complete with hat, walking past his shop and at once phoned Gypsy. She cut him off with, "Oh, John darling, I'm so glad you called. I made a few copies of your marvelous hat, and I need some labels. The hats look so naked without them." The labels arrived shortly. They read: "A Mr. John design stolen by Gypsy Rose Lee."

It's always the badly
dressed people who are
the most interesting.
—*JEAN-PAUL GAULTIER*

A well-tied tie is the
first serious step in life.
—*OSCAR WILDE*
**A WOMAN OF
NO IMPORTANCE**

Clothes make the
man. Naked people
have little or no
influence on society.
—*MARK TWAIN*

You're never fully
dressed without a smile.
—*ANNIE*

Fashion somehow, for me, is purely
and happily irrational.

—HEDI SLIMANE

In difficult times, fashion is always outrageous.

—ELSA SCHIAPARELLI

If loving fashion is a crime, we all plead guilty.

—UNKNOWN

The idea of seeing everybody clad the same is not really my cup of tea.

—*CHRISTIAN LACROIX*

Don't follow [fashion] blindly into every dark alley. Always remember that you are not a model or a mannequin for which the fashion is created.

—*MARLENE DIETRICH*

There is a lot of noise out there. I don't want to follow the trend, I want to create the trend. And talking about trends, I actually have always believed in the saying, "In a world full of trends, I want to remain a classic."

—*IMAN*

A wise friend once told me, "Don't wear what fashion designers tell you to wear. Wear what they wear." His point being that most designers, no matter what they throw onto the runway, favor simple, flattering pieces for themselves.

—TINA FEY

Every generation laughs at the old fashions,
but follows religiously the new.

—HENRY DAVID THOREAU

Fashion consists of imitating what at first seems
to be inimitable.

—ROLAND BARTHES

Like all tyrants, fashion only exercises its power
entirely over those too weak to resist it.

—HONORÉ DE BALZAC

Fashion's authority is so absolute that it forces us to be ridiculous at the risk of seeming it.

—JOSEPH SANIAL-DUBAY

One fashion has scarcely destroyed another before it is overturned by a newer one, which itself yields to the one that follows, which is never the last: such is our fickleness.

—JEAN DE LA BRUYÈRE

Women dress alike all over the world:
They dress to be annoying to other women.

—ELSA SCHIAPARELLI

All women's dresses are merely variations on
the eternal struggle between the admitted desire
to dress and the unadmitted desire to undress.

—LIN YUTANG

Fashion is what one wears oneself. What is unfashionable is what other people wear.

—*OSCAR WILDE*
AN IDEAL HUSBAND

Fashion: the search for a new absurdity.

—*NATALIE CLIFFORD BARNEY*

To call a fashion wearable is the kiss of death. No new fashion worth its salt is ever wearable.

—*EUGENIA SHEPPARD*

I don't want a politician who's thinking about fashion for even one millisecond. It's the same as medical professionals. The idea of a person in a Comme des Garçons humpback dress giving me a colonoscopy is just not groovy.

—SIMON DOONAN

Every designer needs an iconic look. If the *South Park* boys cannot make a recognizable cartoon of you, then you need to up the ante. You need a signature flourish, *non*?

—*SIMON DOONAN*

The hardest thing in fashion is not to be known for a logo, but to be known for a silhouette.

—*GIAMBATTISTA VALLI*

Fashions, after all, are only induced epidemics.

—*GEORGE BERNARD SHAW*

I have become convinced that everything
that is classy doesn't go away.

—ADAM WEST

Fashion is the mirror of history.

—LOUIS XIV OF FRANCE

Be neither too early in the fashion, nor too long
out of it; nor at any time in the extremes of it.

—JOHANN KASPAR LAVATER

I'll have to put more earrings on. I bet that someone could analyze me and tell my condition by my earrings.

—*EDIE SEDGWICK*

I wear my sort of clothes to save me the trouble of deciding which clothes to wear.

—*KATHERINE HEPBURN*

I base my fashion taste on what doesn't itch.

—*GILDA RADNER*

Make it simple, but significant.

—DON DRAPER
MAD MEN

I go back and forth between wanting to be abundantly simple and maddeningly complex.

—JOHN BALDESSARI

Simplicity is the ultimate sophistication.

—LEONARDO DA VINCI

The joy of dressing is an art.

—*JOHN GALLIANO*

Fashion is the armor to survive the reality
of everyday life.

—*BILL CUNNINGHAM*

But if fashion were easy,
wouldn't everybody look great?

—*TIM GUNN*

STYLE AS

ATTITUDE

Be who you are.
Say what you feel.
Wear what you like.
Do what you want.
But make sure you
do it with some style.

The most alluring thing a woman can have
is confidence.

—BEYONCÉ

With hair, heels, and attitude, honey,
I am through the roof.

—RUPAUL

I have never known a really chic woman whose
appearance was not, in large part, an outward
reflection of her inner self.

—MAINBOCHER

Dress like you might run into your worst enemy.

—*KIMORA LEE SIMMONS*

If you're going out at night, for heaven's sake wear something that explodes and goes pow. A dress that doesn't knock-em-dead when you come into a room is absolutely no good these days.

—*NORMAN NORELL*

B e daring, be different, be impractical, be anything that will assert integrity of purpose and imaginative vision against the play-it-safers, the creatures of the commonplace, the slaves of the ordinary.

—*CECIL BEATON*

The Flapper awoke from her lethargy of sub-deb-ism, bobbed her hair, put on her choicest pair of earrings and a great deal of audacity and rouge and went into the battle. She flirted because it was fun to flirt and wore a one-piece bathing suit because she had a good figure, she covered her face with powder and paint because she didn't need it and she refused to be bored chiefly because she wasn't boring. She was conscious that the things she did were the things she had always wanted to do. Mothers disapproved of their sons taking the Flapper to dances, to teas, to swim and most of all to heart. She had mostly masculine friends, but youth does not need friends—it needs only crowds.

—ZELDA FITZGERALD

STYLE IS . . .

. . . when they're running you out of town and you make it look like you're leading the parade.

—*WILLIAM BATTIE*

. . . wearing an evening dress to McDonald's, wearing heels to play football. It is personality, confidence and seduction.

—*JOHN GALLIANO*

. . . a way to say who you are without having to speak.

—*RACHEL ZOE*

. . . whatever you want to do, if you can do it with confidence.

—*GEORGE CLINTON*

. . . the image of character.

—*EDWARD GIBBON*

People should dress the way they want.
Any rules for age or shape are silly.

—*SARAH JESSICA PARKER*

It is what a woman leaves off, not what she puts
on, that gives her cachet.

—*PAUL POIRET*

When a woman smiles, then her dress should smile too.

—*MADELEINE VIONNET*

A fashionable woman is always in love—
with herself.

—*LA ROCHEFOUCAULD*

The beauty of a woman is not in the clothes she wears, the figure that she carries, or the way she combs her hair. The beauty of a woman is seen in her eyes, because that is the doorway to her heart, the place where love resides. True beauty in a woman is reflected in her soul. It's the caring that she lovingly gives, the passion that she shows, and the beauty of a woman only grows with passing years.

—*AUDREY HEPBURN*

Adopting a really positive attitude can work wonders to adding years to your life, a spring to your step, a sparkle to your eye, and all of that.

—*CHRISTIE BRINKLEY*

Age and size are only numbers. It's the attitude you bring to clothes that make the difference.

—*DONNA KARAN*

FINELY WO- VEN SILK

WINSTON CHURCHILL

Winston Churchill lived during the Victorian and Edwardian eras, fought during two world wars, and saw the atomic age before he passed away. He determined that the British would fight the Nazis and raged against anti-Semitism. He was a soldier, a painter, and a reader, and ultimately he won a Nobel Prize in literature. And, according to his wife, he spent a great deal of money on "very finely woven silk (pale pink)" underwear.

Attitude is a little thing that makes a big difference.

—ZIG ZIGLAR

Find out who you are and do it on purpose.

—DOLLY PARTON

Personally, I think that sexy is keeping yourself mysterious. I'm really an old-fashioned girl, and I think I'm totally sexy.

—STEVIE NICKS

Nothing makes a woman more beautiful
than the belief that she is beautiful.

—SOPHIA LOREN

A woman is never sexier than when she is
comfortable in her clothes.

—VERA WANG

Let the others have the beauty.
I've got the charisma.

—CARINE ROITFELD

The elements that create glamour are not specific styles—bias-cut gowns or lacquered furniture—but more general qualities: grace, mystery, transcendence. To the right audience, Halle Berry is more glamorous commanding the elements as Storm in the X-Men movies than she is walking the red carpet in a designer gown.

—*VIRGINIA POSTREL*

To achieve the nonchalance which is absolutely necessary for a man, one article at least must not match.

—*HARDY AMIES*

The style of studied nonchalance is the psychological triumph of grace over order.

—*G. BRUCE BOYER*

Whatever does not pretend at all has style enough.

—*BOOTH TARKINGTON*
THE MAGNIFICENT AMBERSONS

The coolest thing is when you don't care about being cool anymore. Indifference is the greatest aphrodisiac: that's what really sums up style for me.

—*RICK OWENS*

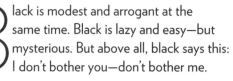lack is modest and arrogant at the same time. Black is lazy and easy—but mysterious. But above all, black says this: I don't bother you—don't bother me.

—*YOHJI YAMAMOTO*

I always feel that if you're gonna be
uncomfortable and unhappy in something,
just because you think it's in or it's chic,
I would advise you to be happy rather than
well-dressed. It's better to be happy.

—IRIS APFEL

If you don't love it, don't get into it! That's my rule.

—CHRISTIAN SIRIANO

Beauty of style and harmony and grace and good rhythm depend on simplicity.

—PLATO

The more you leave out, the more you highlight what you leave in.

—HENRY GREEN

If you're going to do something, do it with style.

—JASON STATHAM

Elegance is elimination.

—CRISTÓBAL BALENCIAGA

Fashion anticipates, and elegance is
a state of mind.

—OLEG CASSINI

When a girl feels that she's perfectly
groomed and dressed she can forget
that part of her. That's charm.

—F. SCOTT FITZGERALD

Italian style is a natural
attitude. It is about
a life of good taste.
It doesn't have to be
expensive. Simple
but with good taste.
Luxury is possible to
buy. Good taste is not.

—*DIEGO DELLA VALLE*

Fake is not chic . . .
but fake fur is.

—*KARL LAGERFELD*

Luxury is less expensive
than elegance.

—*HONORÉ DE BALZAC*

I adore wearing gems,
but not because they
are mine. You can't
possess radiance you
can only admire it.

—*ELIZABETH TAYLOR*

Elegance is usually confused with superficiality, fashion, lack of depth. This is a serious mistake: human beings need to have elegance in their actions and in their posture, because this word is synonymous with good taste, amiability, equilibrium, and harmony.

—PAULO COELHO

Clothes aren't going to change the world,
the women who wear them will.

—ANNE KLEIN

It's all about being comfortable, being easy
and having you be able to wear something and
not having it wear you. It's classic.

—JENNIFER ANISTON

I've always believed in the adage that the secret
of eternal youth is arrested development.

—ALICE ROOSEVELT

I have always believed that clothes are terribly important in every woman's life . . . And I also believe that there is much of beauty in aviation— color and line that is exclusive to the air, which I have attempted to express in sports clothes.

—AMELIA EARHART

Women cherish fashion because it rejuvenates them, or at least renews them.

—MADAME DE PREIZEUX

There are sometimes people, or things, possessed of an invisible charm, a natural grace, that is impossible to define, and that one is forced to call the *je ne sais quoi*.

—MONTESQUIEU

Put even the plainest woman into a beautiful dress and unconsciously she will try to live up to it.

—LADY DUFF-GORDON

People will stare. Make it worth their while.

—HARRY WINSTON

You can have anything you want. If you dress for it.

—EDITH HEAD

Walk like you have three men walking behind you.

—OSCAR DE LA RENTA

Sports clothes changed our lives because they changed our thinking about clothes. Perhaps they, more than anything else, made us independent women. In the days of dependent women—fainting women, delicate flowers, laced to breathless beauty— a girl couldn't cross the street without help. Her mission in life was to look beautiful and seductive while the men took care of the world's problems. Today women can share the problems (and possibly help with them) because of their new-found freedom.

—CLAIRE MCCARDELL

Girls do not dress for boys. They dress for themselves, of course. If girls dressed for boys, they'd just walk around naked all the time.

—*BETSEY JOHNSON*

Being a sex symbol has to do with an attitude, not looks. Most men think it's looks; most women know otherwise.

—*KATHLEEN TURNER*

Think pink, as Diana Vreeland said.
But don't wear it!

—*KARL LAGERFELD*

Pearls are always appropriate.

—*JACKIE KENNEDY*

Be eccentric now. Don't wait for old age
to wear purple.

—*REGINA BRETT*

I can wear a hat or take it off, but either way it's a conversation piece.

—HEDDA HOPPER

For beautiful eyes, look for the good in others; for beautiful lips, speak only words of kindness; and for poise, walk with the knowledge that you are never alone.

—*SAM LEVENSON*

When you incline to have new clothes, look first well over the old ones, and see if you cannot shift with them another year, either by scouring, mending, or even patching if necessary. Remember, a patch on your coat, and money in your pocket, is better and more creditable, than a writ on your back, and no money to take it off.

—BENJAMIN FRANKLIN

DIANA,
PRINCESS
OF WALES

THE
PEOPLE'S
PRIN-
CESS

Throughout her life, Diana, Princess of Wales, was known for both her fashion and humanitarian efforts, two passions she found unique and beautiful ways to combine. Her colorful clothes were carefully chosen to emphasize her warmth and openness. She abstained from royal tradition and often skipped wearing gloves so she could hold the hands of those she met. She intentionally chose chunky jewelry more appealing to children, meant for them to play with. Even the fabrics and textiles she wore showcased her thoughtful and caring nature. She specifically dressed in a tactile fabric like velvet while visiting hospitals for the blind—actions truly emblematic of the people's princess.

I don't find clothes sexy at all. I find people sexy.

—MARC JACOBS

The height of sophistication is simplicity.

—CLARE BOOTHE LUCE
STUFFED SHIRTS

Style is just the outside of content, and content the inside of style, like the outside and the inside of the human body both go together, they can't be separated.

—JEAN-LUC GODARD

Why don't I just step out and slip into something more spectacular?

—LIBERACE

Conformity is the only real fashion crime. To not dress like yourself and to sublimate your spirit to some kind of group identity is succumbing to fashion fascism.

—SIMON DOONAN

Over the years I have learned that what is important in a dress is the woman who is wearing it.

—*YVES SAINT LAURENT*

LIFE IN

STYLE

Style is not only
what we wear, it's an
extension of and insight
into who we are. But
more than that, our lives
are even fuller when
lived with style.

You gotta have style. It helps you get down
the stairs, it helps you get up in the morning.
It's a way of life. Without it you're nobody.

—*DIANA VREELAND*

Being perfectly well-dressed gives a feeling
of inward tranquility which religion is powerless
to bestow.

—*RALPH WALDO EMERSON*

Putting on a beautifully designed suit elevates
my spirit, extols my sense of self, and helps
define me as a man to whom details matter.

—*GAY TALESE*

Every minute of every hour of every day you are making the world, just as you are making yourself, and you might as well do it with generosity and kindness and style.

—*REBECCA SOLNIT*

All of us invent ourselves. Some of us just have more imagination than others.

—*CHER*

Style is knowing who you are, what you want to say, and not giving a damn.

—*GORE VIDAL*

Style isn't just about what you wear,
it's about how you live.

—LILLY PULITZER

Fashion isn't just frocks. It's how we do our
houses, our gardens, it's what we eat and drink.

—GRACE CODDINGTON

QUEEN ELIZABETH II

THE PRINCESS SAVED

Princess Elizabeth, future monarch of England, wore a stunning silk gown on her wedding day. Embroidered with white seed pearls from America and featuring crystals, silver thread, and appliqué tulle embroidery, the dress was designed by Norman Hartnell and drew inspiration from Botticelli's *Primavera*. England was still recovering from the financial stresses of World War II at the time, and the princess notably saved ration cards in order to pay for its making.

If at first you don't succeed, failure may be your style.

—*QUENTIN CRISP*

For me, music and life are all about style.

—*MILES DAVIS*

In character, in manner, in style, in all things,
the supreme excellence is simplicity.

—*HENRY WADSWORTH LONGFELLOW*
KAVANAGH

Dressing well is a form of good manners.

—*TOM FORD*

Any man may be in good spirits and
good temper when he's well dressed.

—*CHARLES DICKENS*
**THE LIFE AND ADVENTURES
OF MARTIN CHUZZLEWIT**

Keeping your clothes well pressed will
keep you from looking hard pressed.

—*COLEMAN COX*

Life's too short to wear boring clothes.

—*CARLY CUSHNIE
AND MICHELLE OCHS*

Don't be into trends. Don't make fashion own you, but you decide what you are, what you want to express by the way you dress and the way you live.

—*GIANNI VERSACE*

Don't just steal the style, steal the thinking behind the style. You don't want to look like your heroes, you want to see like your heroes.

—*AUSTIN KLEON*
STEAL LIKE AN ARTIST

Be sure what you want and be sure about yourself. Fashion is not just beauty, it's about good attitude. You have to believe in yourself and be strong.

—ADRIANA LIMA

His are the only clothes in which I am myself. He is far more than a couturier, he is a creator of personality.

—AUDREY HEPBURN
on Hubert de Givenchy

It's the ugly things I notice more, because
other people tend to ignore the ugly things.

—ALEXANDER MCQUEEN

You can't eat beauty, it doesn't feed you . . .
beauty was not a thing that I could acquire or
consume, it was something that I just had to be.

—LUPITA NYONG'O

I don't think I was born beautiful.
I just think I was born me.

—NAOMI CAMPBELL

I think in black.

—GARETH PUGH

I wore black because I liked it. I still do and wearing
it still means something to me. It's still my symbol
of rebellion—against a stagnant status quo, against
our hypocritical houses of God, against people
whose minds are closed to others' ideas.

—JOHNNY CASH

Women who wear black lead
colorful lives.

—*NEIMAN MARCUS*

ELIZABETH TAYLOR

DIA-MONDS WON'T KEEP YOU WARM AT NIGHT

Richard Burton once bought a Cartier diamond for Elizabeth Taylor for $1.1 million. "I wanted that diamond because it is incomparably lovely," Burton said. "And it should be on the loveliest woman in the world."

Taylor was significantly more than a fashion and style icon, though, and her successes as an actress and a humanitarian were equally important to her character. "You can't cry on a diamond's shoulder, and diamonds won't keep you warm at night," she said. "But they're sure fun when the sun shines."

The subject may be crude and repulsive.
Its expression is artistically modulated and
balanced. This is style. This is art.

—*VLADIMIR NABOKOV*

With confidence, I think anyone can get
a dress and make it their own. I don't think you
should have it off the runway and wear it like
they want you to wear it. You know, with their hair
and makeup—their woman. I just think it's boring.
You have to make it your own. That's what
fashion is all about.

—*KATE MOSS*

Vain trifles as they seem, clothes have, they say, more important offices than to merely keep us warm. They change our view of the world and the world's view of us.

—*VIRGINIA WOOLF*
ORLANDO

I don't believe in fashion. I believe in costume. Life is too short to be the same person every day.

—*STEPHANIE PERKINS*
LOLA AND THE BOY NEXT DOOR

On Wednesdays, we wear pink!

—MEAN GIRLS

Pink isn't a color, it's an attitude!

—*MILEY CYRUS*

Pink is not a color—it's a culture to me.

—*DEANGELO WILLIAMS*

Anyone can get dressed up and glamorous,
but it is how people dress in their days off
that are the most intriguing.

—ALEXANDER WANG

You can find inspiration in everything.
If you can't, then you're not looking properly.

—PAUL SMITH

Real fashion change comes from real changes
in real life. Everything else is just decoration.

—TOM FORD

Concision in style, precision in thought,
decision in life.

—*VICTOR HUGO*

On matters of style, swim with the current,
on matters of principle, stand like a rock.

—*THOMAS JEFFERSON*

Know first who you are, and then adorn
yourself accordingly.

—*EPICTETUS*

Being happy never goes out of style.

—LILLY PULITZER

I make style out of life, not style out of style.

—ISSEY MIYAKE

We all put obstacles in our own path toward personal style, myself included. If we understood why we constructed these practical and emotional obstacles, we might move beyond it to healthier, happier perceptions of ourselves and, ideally, a better sense of self-esteem.

—STACY LONDON

When I design and wonder what the point is, I think of someone having a bad time in their life. Maybe they are sad and they wake up and put on something I have made and it makes them feel just a bit better. So, in that sense, fashion is a little help in the life of a person. But only a little.

—MIUCCIA PRADA

Taking sartorial risks and not following
other people is what makes you stand out.

—*ZAC POSEN*

If you've got it, wear it.

—*LOUIS MOUNTBATTEN'S*
advice to Prince Charles

If you wear things you adore, you just look better.

—*MARGHERITA MISSONI*

want to be different.
If everyone is wearing black,
I want to be wearing red.

—MARIA SHARAPOVA

Style—all who have it have one thing: originality.

—DIANA VREELAND

The original style is not the style which never borrows of any one, but that which no other person is capable of reproducing.

—FRANÇOIS-RENÉ,
VICOMTE DE CHATEAUBRIAND

Sometimes you have to play a long time
to be able to play like yourself.

—MILES DAVIS

You don't have to have one personal style,
and you needn't stick to it for life, either.

—JOE ZEE

The most important thing to remember is that you can wear all the greatest clothes and all the greatest shoes, but you've got to have a good spirit on the inside. That's what's really going to make you look like you're ready to rock the world.

—ALICIA KEYS

My mission in life is not merely
to survive, but to thrive; and
to do so with some passion, some
compassion, some humor, and some style.

—MAYA ANGELOU

Design by Hana Anouk Nakamura
Custom Typography by Nick Misani

ISBN: 978-1-4197-3398-7

Foreword © 2019 Isabelle Thomas

© 2019 Abrams

Printed and bound in China
10 9 8 7 6 5 4 3 2 1

Abrams Noterie products are available at special discounts when
purchased in quantity for premiums and promotions as well as
fundraising or educational use. Special editions can also be created
to specification. For details, contact specialsales@abramsbooks.com
or the address below.

ABRAMS The Art of Books
195 Broadway, New York, NY 10007
abramsbooks.com